Prairie Spirits

Ghost Stories and Hauntings at the

Red Brick School & Oppertshauser House

In Stony Plain, Alberta

By Alexis Marie Chute

Copyright © 2021 Alexis Marie Chute

All rights reserved. No part of this publication may be reproduced, distributed, or transmitted in any form or by any means, including photocopying, recording, digital scanning, or other electronic or mechanical methods, without the prior written permission of the publisher, except in the case of brief quotations embodied in critical reviews and certain other non-commercial uses permitted by copyright law. For permission requests, please address Wild Skies Press.

Published 2021
Printed in Canada

ISBN Print 978-0-9950788-0-2
ISBN eBook 978-0-9950788-1-9

Cover Design by Alexis Marie Chute
Interior Design by Alexis Marie Chute

For information address:
Wild Skies Press
A division of Alexis Marie Productions Inc.
Edmonton, Alberta, Canada
info@alexismariechute.com
www.WildSkiesPress.com

Wild Skies Press is an independent literary publisher founded in 2021. Wild Skies refers to the aurora borealis—northern lights—in Alberta, where the press is located, situated on Treaty 6 Territory. Wild Skies Press publishes non-fiction, fiction, poetry, and hybrid genres and artforms with an emphasis on the creation of Canadian works and books by emerging and established authors. **www.WildSkiesPress.com**

Table of Contents

Introduction 1
A Brief History of the Buildings 5
Ghost Profiles 13

Ghost Stories and Hauntings 17
      Schoolhouse Hauntings 22
      Oppertshauser House Hauntings 32

Interviews & Firsthand Accounts 39
      Angela Fetch Muzyka 42
      Sandra Teves 48
      Twyla McGann 51
      Jodi Frechette 58
      Erin Greaves 72
      Victoria Marsh 77
      Sal K. 83

Paranormal Investigations 86
      Ghost Hunting Tools 89
      Investigation: ParanorBill 93
      Investigation: The Alberta Paranormal Investigators Society 99

Ghost Tour 108

About the Multicultural Heritage Centre 114
Author Acknowledgments 117
Author Bio 119
References & Sources 122

Introduction

When I began working as Art Curator at the Multicultural Heritage Centre in January 2020, I was thrilled to spend time in the gorgeous historic Red Brick Schoolhouse in Stony Plain, Alberta. The art gallery is in one of the old classrooms that in later years occasionally functioned as the gymnasium. At the first exhibit opening I organized, the current and former animators, Twyla McGann and Angela Fetch Muzyka, were both in attendance. Once the exhibit guests departed for the evening and the party food and supplies were put away, Twyla and Angela illuminated for me the history of both the school building and Oppertshauser House that share the landscaped garden at the Centre.

"The buildings are haunted, you know." I can't recall if it was Twyla or Angela who said this. I did not, in fact, know that information. The women educated me on the stories they had heard from other staff and visitors, plus their own experiences while on the grounds and in the buildings.

Easily creeped out, I was eager to lock-up and head home, but they guided me back into the art gallery. The lights were off. Only the warm glow of streetlamps shone through the windows, casting long shadows on the creaking maple floor and art-covered walls around us. Was this a ritual initiation to working at the Centre? The serious expressions on Twyla's and Angela's faces told me that this was no joke.

Twyla instructed me to listen, saying, "I often hear murmured talking." We were the last ones in the building. My chest was still as I held my breath, but I doubt I would have heard anything beyond my heart pounding against my ribs.

Standing there, book-ended by two sensible women I much admired, I wondered at their firm belief in their strange experiences. True, with the lights out I could imagine catching a glimpse of a smoky apparition inhabiting one of the old buildings. Every psychic who visited the Centre over the years had agreed: spirits dwell there. Some have sensed as many as seven ghosts. At the very least, three: a woman, a man, and a child.

I have probably watched too many horror movies in my youth to imagine a peaceful encounter with the dead—but that is exactly what happens at the Centre. Angela and Twyla assured me that their encounters with the "other side" have never felt malicious or evil. The ghosts are tricksters, playing pranks and making themselves known. No one has ever been hurt, although many have been scared senseless.

I didn't hear voices that night in the gallery, but I did have my own spooky incident when recreating specific scenes to photograph for this book. Two actors in period costumes were helping me create an image in the upstairs of the Oppertshauser House. The male actor, Ethan, stood in the closet where lore tells us a young man took his own life decades ago. The female actor, Nicole, shone a light on the side of Ethan's face and I clicked my camera as a smoke machine pumped out a creeping mist. The fire alarm went off in the hall and moments later firefighters arrived. I explained what we were up to, and they gave us advice to cover the fire detector with plastic and tape it to the ceiling, which we did.

Stony Plain firefighters who rushed to the Centre when the fire alarm went off during a photo shoot recreating a scene in the Oppertshauser House. August 2021. Photo shared with permission.

Ethan, Nicole, and I went back to our scene. This time, the smoke detector in the children's bedroom went off. We covered our ears against the blaring beeps and Ethan, being the tallest, pulled the unit off the ceiling and popped out the batteries. We three stood there, mouths agape, as the alarm continued to blare. I was gobsmacked. How was the detector continuing to beep without a power source? Had I finally encountered the Centre's paranormal for myself? The remnants of smoke wafted around us and our blood ran cold in those moments.

Research following that day has informed me that smoke detectors can hold a charge for a short while after their batteries are removed, and old units can be triggered by dust touching the battery plates. My electrician cousin and the Centre's groundskeeper, both sensible handymen, assured me there was nothing spooky about my experience. While my mind relents to logic, my gut tells me otherwise. Which do I trust?

If you are a skeptic, perhaps the stories in this book will come off as coincidental anomalies or explainable phenomena. Maybe you will concede that so many accounts corroborate that something unusual has taken place at the Centre. If you are a believer with stories of your own, these documented experiences might be further evidence for your faith in what cannot be seen or rationalized.

No matter what you believe, I hope these stories entertain you. I invite you to visit Stony Plain and the Multicultural Heritage Centre to make up your own mind on these otherworldly matters.

A Brief History of The Buildings

Red Brick Schoolhouse. Multicultural Heritage Centre Archives, Photographer Unknown

Red Brick Schoolhouse

Designed by Blakey, Blakey, and Symonds, an Edmonton architectural firm, the red brick structure takes design inspiration from the 19th century British Arts and Crafts Movement, typical of the late Victorian era. A bell tower rises above a hip-and-gable roof clad in cedar shakes, and the building's many windows are trimmed in brilliant white. A large sign above the main entrance reads, "STONY PLAIN SCHOOL."

Built in 1925 in the middle of a farmer's field, this was the first regional school in Stony Plain. It filled the needs of the rural area's growing population resulting from European immigration after World War One and entrepreneurial folks wishing to start businesses and farms outside the city. Many of the first homes built surrounding the schoolhouse were for boarding teachers and students.

The school's first principal was Ted Kibblewhite, and typically no more than two additional teachers were on staff at a time: one designated to the Sciences, the other to the Humanities.

> **"There was no other building like it in Canada.
> It was the most impractical school ever built."**
>
> —*Mr. F. P. Flanagan*
> *Teacher and Principal for 17 years*

Two classrooms on the main floor of the schoolhouse accommodated children of all ages, with the youngsters sitting in the front and the older students in the back. The school sometimes served as overflow for students from other community schools.

The upper floor was initially not used for classrooms, as the stairs were narrow and steep. The space instead functioned as a changing area, storage space, and the student infirmary. In 1937, with the purchase of five typewriters, it became a clerical studies lab. Other vocational classes, such as Shop and Home Economics, were taught on the lower-level in the walkout basement.

*Red Brick Schoolhouse. Multicultural Heritage Centre Archives,
Photographer Unknown*

The school operated until 1949, transitioning briefly into an occupational training centre before falling into neglect and decay for a decade. The schoolhouse was purchased in 1974 by the Heritage Agricultural Society and renovated to become a Provincial Historic Site in 1983.

In 1974, the Homesteader's Kitchen opened in what was the Home Economics classroom. The restaurant space would change business names and chefs numerous times. Today it is known as Wheet Nothings Gluten Free Diner. One of the main floor classrooms, which might have served as a gymnasium in later years, is now the public art gallery. The other instructional room has been

revived as a Pioneer Cabin living museum. The upper floor houses a library and a museum displaying the history of the building and the town.

The Oppertshauser House

The Oppertshauser House was originally built in what is now a residential neighbourhood and business district of Stony Plain. Henry Oppertshauser Sr. took inspiration from European design and the building remains mostly unchanged from its 1910 construction, except for the summer kitchen built in 1913.

Oppertshauser House. Multicultural Heritage Centre Archives, Photographer Unknown

Henry Sr. lived there only a few years before he gave the house to his son George and daughter-in-law, Barbara, in 1912. The couple raised their three children—Walter, Louise, and Oscar—in the house and lived there until 1968. The Oppertshauser family was heavily involved in the early development of the community and often hosted gatherings in their home.

Kathy Ducholke, an Oppertshauser descendant, rented out the home until 1984, then sold it to the Heritage Agricultural Society in January of 1985. With nearly $100,000 in fundraising dollars, the building was relocated to its new foundation in 1987. The Oppertshauser House's first address, 5019-51 Avenue, is only a two-minute drive from where it now stands. The front of the summer kitchen was restored after the move and the exterior updated with a sign from the family business, "Oppertshauser Hardware Store."

The Oppertshauser House has had many iterations over the years at the Centre. Its main floor was once an art gallery and later the General Store gift shop. The upper floor was staff offices for a time. The basement was and remains museum storage, archives, and office space. The main floor and upstairs are now a living museum featuring vintage and archival objects placed in the context that the Oppertshauser family might have had them while living there. The house is also used for historical purposes and ghost tours.

Oppertshauser House. Multicultural Heritage Centre Archives, Photographer Unknown

Ghost Profiles

George Oppertshauser
1885–1970

George was the sixth child of Henry Sr. and Elizabeth Oppertshauser. The couple had sixteen children in total, however only thirteen survived their infancies. Henry Sr. had emigrated from Oberglee, Germany to Elmira, Ontario in 1871 before settling in Stony Plain, Alberta.

As a young man, George was a member of the Red Onion Crew with whom he frequently participated in pranks alongside his fellow bachelors. He married Barbara in 1910 and they moved into the original Oppertshauser House after his father built a larger home next door.

George operated the family business, the Oppertshauser Hardware Store, which he took over from his father and managed until his death in 1970. Outside of work, George was busy in community affairs, such as Town Council and the local school board, and he acted as an elder and secretary of St. Matthew's Lutheran Church. He was an avid car enthusiast and golfer, and a founder of the first Stony Plain golf course on the Fairgrounds.

Barbara Oppertshauser
1891–1977

Barbara Ulmer worked in the restaurant at the Royal Hotel, later renamed the Stony Hotel. She married George Oppertshauser on January 2, 1910, and they had three children together. Barbara was active in the community, involved in the local church, and a member and the first treasurer of St. Matthew's Ladies Aid. She outlived George and all her children: two sons Walter and Oscar, her daughter Louise (married name Ducholke), and her daughter-in-law Linda, who was Oscar's wife.

Following George's passing, Barbara lived in the local Good Samaritan senior's home until her death.

Cornelia Railey Wood
1892–1985

Cornelia Railey became a schoolteacher at the age of sixteen and went on to a wide variety of pursuits, including sports, acting, horse riding, and interior decorating. She was also an artist, homemaker, and world traveller. She worked in politics for twenty-seven years, serving as Stony Plain MLA from 1940–1968 and Mayor from 1953–1955.

She helped start the Stony Plain Library, was a charter member of the Alberta Women's Institute, and an accomplished philanthropist. Her books and other archives from her life, including her famous hat collection, are on display at the Centre. She was known to some as, "The lady with the hats," or, "The Hat Lady."

Suicide Victim
Years unknown

Lore tells us that one of George and Barbara's sons, perhaps Walter, took his own life by hanging himself in the upstairs closet of the Oppertshauser House. There is no known documentation to prove this.

Little Girl
Circa 1920s

Individuals and investigators have sensed a young female ghost on the grounds. She may have been a schoolgirl attending classes, or a child who died when the building became a quarantine site during a scarlet fever outbreak around 1921.

Teacher
Circa 1920s

Along with the little girl, there have been reports of a female teacher who died on the grounds. Her death might have been from the flu or scarlet fever, or another cause altogether.

According to urban legend, the teacher took refuge from a blizzard in the school where she taught, and later passed away. No documentation, newspaper coverage, or other proof of the teacher's death in the building was found although multiple individuals have seen a ghostly woman looking out the windows of the schoolhouse.

Ghost Stories & Hauntings

I researched the spooky past and present of the Red Brick Schoolhouse and the Oppertshauser House in a variety of ways. There was much digging through historic records, newspaper articles, emails, old and new ghost tour scripts, and other documentation. This might conjure the image of a curious journalist milling through decaying boxes, dust wafting from aged papers and photographs. What is closer to the truth, however, is a modern-day sleuth, face illuminated by the glowing computer screen. Thankfully, history has been digitized and made more accessible, which is something I hope this book will do for all the stories that have been passed down over the years and shared with me over a cup of coffee or while strolling through the grounds and buildings or presented informally in my own new-employee initiation.

As a part of my research, I studied paranormal investigation videos filmed at the Centre. I learned not only the energetic hot spots to write about, but also the lingo and tools of the ghost-hunting trade. Over the course of two months, I interviewed individuals in person, on video chat, on the phone, and by email, collecting firsthand accounts of otherworldly lore featuring the Multicultural Heritage Centre.

Through this investigation, both the documented history and the word-of-mouth accounts, I have pieced together the stories from this quiet setting in Stony Plain, Alberta.

Schoolhouse Hauntings

Red Brick Schoolhouse

Strange stories abound at the Red Brick Schoolhouse. Staff members have noticed lights on through the school's windows, even after shutting down the building for the night, and misty white figures have been spotted in the main part of the school. Nicole Rees, a summer student at the Centre, said that whenever she spends time in the Red Brick Schoolhouse, she feels nauseated and must quickly leave.

A staff member reported smelling tobacco in the building, though she was alone, and no windows were open. While this event naturally unnerved her, there might be a rational explanation. A newspaper article entitled, "Ghost Tours Offer a Haunting History," published in the *Grove Examiner* on October 27, 2017, captures Angela Fetch Muzyka's thoughts on this.

She is quoted saying, "The big common [ghost story] is people smelling smoke. They forget that these old buildings, especially ones that have wood floors, smells seep into the wood and get stored there. When the buildings shift because of weather changes, you'll experience those smells coming out because of the shifting of the boards releasing something that's been stored there for a long time. There are definitely things that are not paranormal that people equate with being paranormal."

A "Town Board" in the Pioneer Cabin displays local articles and advertisements from the 1921 editions of the *Stony Plain Sun*. There is also a notice that scarlet fever was reported in the region, published by the Medical Authority of Alberta. Multiple deaths have been speculated to have occurred in the school, possibly due to scarlet fever or even the flu, which were deadly at that time in history. These reports lend weight to the ghost stories that a young girl and a female teacher haunt the building.

Front Desk

The front desk has been a hub of spooky happenings, manifested predominantly in technology anomalies. Angela, a former receptionist and museum animator, frequently answered the phone only to find there was no one on the other end of the line, and not even a dial tone. She noticed that these phantom phone calls happened with greater frequency when certain visitors entered the building.

The staff supposed the calls were a glitch with the phone itself. No one could figure it out. With the installation of modern phones equipped with call display, the number of phantom calls per day decreased, but they didn't stop.

When a new staff member took the job, she expected the odd calls after hearing Angela's reports. Instead, she was welcomed into her position by her computer monitor turning itself off periodically. The current receptionist, Sandra Teves, also shared an unnerving happening with her computer. She returned to work one morning to find her computer logged in and the icons on her desktop rearranged. Diligent at signing-out each night, Sandra asked the other staff if any of them had signed on to her computer and none had.

Homesteader's Kitchen

Many businesses have used the kitchen over the years, including a Centre-operated restaurant, and bakeries run by outside contractors. A young chef saw a woman in what she thought was a 1920s period costume. The woman, who the chef spotted out of the corner of her eye, wore a white dress with her hair in a bun, *Little House on the Prairie* style. Others have experienced such mischievous activity as flour mysteriously spilled on the floor, supplies falling from shelves, and footsteps from the floor above early in the morning before anyone else had arrived at the Centre.

One staff member, Gabbie, repeatedly saw the teacher who supposedly died in the schoolhouse a hundred years before, as well as a child. The teacher's ghost would follow Gabbie throughout the building. Gabbie was observed stopping suddenly on the spot or hurrying away. To the other staff, it appeared as if Gabbie was avoiding or fleeing something they could not see. One night, Gabbie got into her car only to find one of the ghosts in her front seat. This has led many at the Centre to advise ghost tour participants to thank the spirits for sharing their space but informing them that they cannot travel home with them that night.

Rebecca, a former Museum Manager at the Centre, reported her own incident from one summer evening. She had been in the basement kitchen preparing to turn on the building's alarm when she heard the back door slam and footsteps sound on the floor above. She supposed someone had entered the old schoolhouse, but when she went upstairs to check no one was there. She returned to the lower level, but the alarm would not arm. It indicated that there was "activity" at the back door. Unnerved, Rebecca departed through the kitchen exit, leaving the building unarmed that night.

Down the hall from the kitchen and main dining area is additional restaurant seating and a gallery where a maintenance woman reported an incident. She was cleaning the room, left to fetch something, and upon her return discovered the tables had been rearranged in her absence.

On one blisteringly cold winter night, a janitor named Brian mopped the hallway between the kitchen and the dining gallery, humming away as he cleaned alone. He popped into the mechanical room near the stairs to dispose of the dirty water. When he returned to the hall, his mouth fell open in shock. There, on the still glistening-wet floor, was a trail of snowy footprints.

There have been many reports of chairs being moved on the lower level of the Red Brick Schoolhouse. A former director found the chairs in the dining gallery stacked and pushed up against the wall every time she needed to have a gathering or board meeting in that room. She grew annoyed to be constantly setting up the meeting space. Confronting the receptionist at the time, she said, "Why do you keep moving the chairs up against the wall?" The receptionist replied, "What are you talking about?" No one knew who was continually tidying the room.

Pioneer Cabin

A past employee at the Centre, Erin Green, told a story to Barbara Smith, author of *More Ghost Stories of Alberta*. It was the story of a local artisan chef who conducted a cooking class in the Cabin. She hauled in multiple loads of her specialty equipment and taught her class, but strange things began happening once her participants had departed for the night. As she was packing up, she noticed the temperature steadily dropping until the room felt icy cold. She then had the eerie sensation of someone standing behind her, staring at the back of her neck. Completely unnerved, she felt an overwhelming urge to exit, which she did, bolting out of the building and leaving behind some of her equipment. The following day she phoned the Centre and explained what had happened, stating that she refused to ever return. The Centre had to deliver her abandoned cooking supplies.

In 2018, a mystic accompanied the Centre's ghost tours, and led the guests in a supernatural exercise while in the Cabin. Multiple individuals—on separate tour evenings, completely independent of each other—reported that following the exercise they sensed a shadowy presence in the northeast corner of the room. They all felt uneasy in that spot, though none could elaborate beyond the word "shadowy."

Archives and Library

According to folklore, back when the building was a school, a housekeeper lived in the attic. Some have claimed to hear a rocking chair creaking back and forth from that space under the rafters.

Robin Lillywhite worked in the Red Brick Schoolhouse for his first four years of twelve at the Centre. He frequently heard the sound of phantom footsteps on the stairs leading to the top floor. He would also feel a presence as if he were not alone, and an overwhelming urge to leave. "I can't stress that enough," he said of the compulsion to vacate the building.

Derek Harrison was the first Executive Director at the Centre. His office was in the present-day Library and Archives room. "That's where things got weird," Robin said of the space. He shared a story where Derek was working late and saw a floating woman in front of a bookshelf. Another time Derek reported feeling the hairs on the back of his neck stand up straight when he was near the attic access across the hall from his office.

Many years ago, two photo albums were donated to the Centre along with other documents. Records indicate that these photographs captured the grand opening of the Multicultural Heritage Centre. These albums were stored in the Archives room where two staff members catalogued historical documents and artifacts. One day, they discovered that the albums had disappeared. Questioning each other, accusations flew back and forth as to who had removed them, both denying it fervently. The albums were missing for two years until an electrician fixing wire in the attic discovered them tucked between two beams.

Folklore tells us that the ghost of Cornelia Wood often visits the top floor of the schoolhouse. There, a display in her honour stands behind glass. She is celebrated as a pioneering women's rights advocate and politician in Stony Plain. Part of the display presents Cornelia's famous hat collection. Does the Hat Lady's spirit visit the school to check on her collection? Some visitors and staff believe so. Other lore states that Cornelia has been seen on the grounds—wearing a hat of course. One report by an unknown individual alleges that they heard her speak in their head, scolding children not to ride their bikes too fast on the path.

Art Gallery

While installing a new exhibit one evening years ago, art gallery curator Lucille listened to *Serial*, a podcast discussing cold case murders. She ascended a ladder to hang an artwork, then felt an unexpected shove from behind. She gasped and clutched the ladder to avoid losing her footing. No one was there. She descended the ladder, trembling. Lucille later reflected that perhaps the subject matter of the podcast had upset a ghostly presence in the room. From that day on she stopped listening to *Serial* and ensured she was never alone in the art gallery. This is one of the only accounts of supernatural activity at the Centre that might have resulted in injury.

Staff working in the kitchen report hearing walking and running footsteps above them in the gallery at all hours of the day. One night, a woman was cooking when she heard distinct footsteps in the art gallery. She texted Twyla McGann, the museum curator at the time, asking her if she was repairing the gallery walls or hanging a new show.

Twyla replied, "Nope, I'm at home in my pyjamas." In my interview with Twyla, she said she didn't think the gallery was ever a gymnasium, as the ghostly running footsteps might suggest and as I had heard elsewhere—unless, she supposed, it was when the building accommodated the overflow from other community schools.

Oppertshauser House Hauntings

The Oppertshauser House is old, and with age comes the expected creeks and groans. However, the spooky stories extend far beyond these normal occurrences. There have been reports of unusual pockets of cold air. The front door swings open by itself without cause. When lone staff members work late, they hear doors slam in other parts of the house, solidifying the heebie-jeebies in generations of employees.

People see small orbs of light wafting through the air. During ghost tours, the house lights flash, dim, or simply go out. Some see full body apparitions in period clothing or silhouettes in the windows. The security system detects motion inside the house, the alarm company will call, the police or fire department will arrive and inspect, but there will be no one within.

The wooden stairs leading to the bedrooms will creek even when no one is on them. Can this be attributed to the settling of the historic building? Perhaps. But what about the sounds of music that have been reported in the house? There is a piano in the living room and an old gramophone stands in a corner of the dining room. The Oppertshauser family were known for being musical, not to mention very social, hosting parties with boisterous conversation and music. Who's to say they are not also sociable in death?

Robin Lillywhite spent his final eight years at the Centre working in the Oppertshauser House. This was during the time the upper floor housed staff offices. One of the employees' traditions at that time was to "say 'good morning' to the ghosts." Robin said, "If you didn't, something would go wrong. Something would go missing." He would always wonder if it was coincidental or if George's ghost was up to his antics again. Robin worked with three others in the upstairs offices. "95 percent of the staff I've worked with [at the Centre] experienced something unexplainable." Robin described the Oppertshauser House as an "active" haunt.

One afternoon, the Town of Stony Plain took a photograph of Judy Unterschultz, Executive Director at the Centre while Robin worked there, standing in front of the Oppertshauser House. The photo showed something visible in the upstairs window. That was Robin's office, and no one was in the building at the time the picture was taken.

Main Floor

The main floor of the Oppertshauser House was an artisan store and gift shop for many years. Multiple employees have described unusual occurrences in that space, such as store objects rearranged or misplaced, the smell of tobacco smoke—George Oppertshauser was an avid pipe smoker—and sounds of movement on the floor above. George was known as a prankster in his bachelor days with his friends in the Red Onion Crew, and the staff typically assume the odd occurrences are his mischievous spirit at play.

In the shop, there was a farm animal play set for sale. A staff member named Victoria would intentionally rearrange the set, leaving the farm animals outside the coral. She closed the shop at night, and the next morning the tiny animals had returned to their places within the miniature fence by the barn.

One night, Victoria thought she'd test her theory further. She placed the animals all around the shop, on different shelves and countertops. When she returned the next morning, all the animals were back within the coral and were facing the door where she stood. Victoria vowed never to upset the display—or the spirits—again.

Gloria, another staff member in the old General Store, noticed a set of nesting dolls rock back and forth on a shelf. There was no wind. No one had bumped the display. Gloria investigated the floorboards. Was there a rattle in the house that cause the dolls to become unbalanced? Nope. Was there a draft from the heater or air conditioner? No. Even when Gloria moved the nesting dolls to a new location in the store, the phenomenon continued.

One summer day, Nicole Rees was co-leading a summer camp at the Centre for children between the ages of five and twelve. They were sitting on the floor in the dining room of the Oppertshauser House when they heard an old-style phone ring to life. *Ring, ring*. The first ring broke through the children's chatter. The second pierced the silence as the group looked around at each other to find the source of the sound. Nicole and the other camp leaders did not have their cell phones with them. They checked the historic phone by the door. It had never been connected to an outlet. They never discovered the source of the ringing. The campers, as unnerved as Nicole and the other leaders, swiftly exited the building.

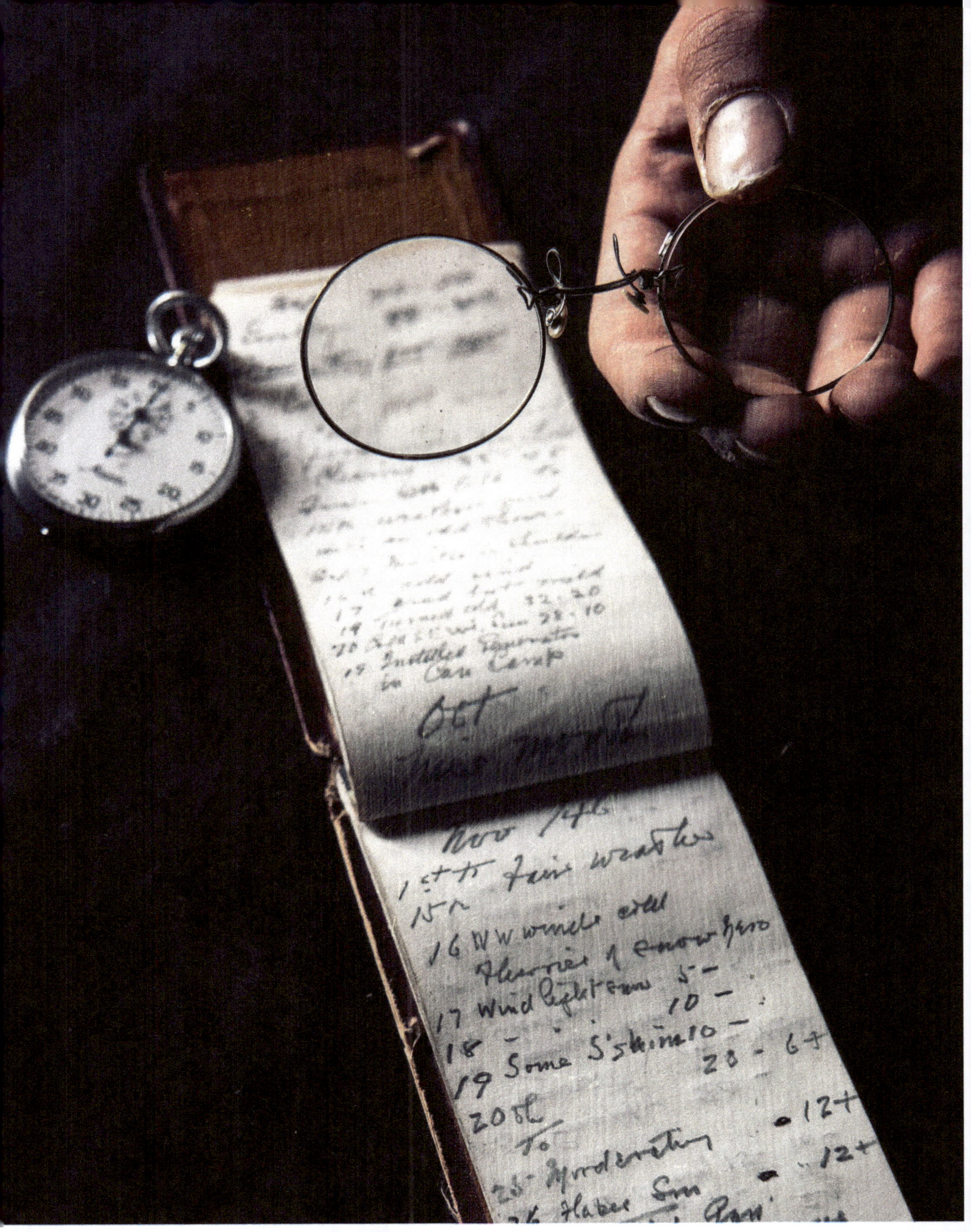

fair weather
Some
Moderating

Upstairs Bedrooms

Ellen Green, was at her desk in one of the Oppertshauser House bedrooms one day when a visitor struck up a conversation, telling Ellen that her mother once worked as a cleaner in the old house. As a child, the visitor would occasionally accompany her mother on the job. The encounter wasn't odd in and of itself, but as soon as the woman left, Ellen smelled men's cologne. Other staff members confirmed the smell. Ellen told Barbara Smith, author of *More Ghost Stories of Alberta*, "I think the woman's visit caused some sort of disturbance in the force."

Early one Saturday morning, another employee heard noises coming from upstairs. "Hello? Is anyone there?" she called up the staircase, but there was no response. Moments later, once she returned to her task, the sound of movements above resumed. Partly in jest, she asked the air, "George, if that's you, give me a sign." Suddenly, there was a loud stomp at the top of the stairs.

It is not only the staff who experience the supernatural in the Oppertshauser house. Many individuals tell stories of their visits, however some never speak of the house again, like one curious man. He entered the building and asked the staffer if it was haunted. Whether he inquired in seriousness or humour, the answer he received was a resounding, "YES." He ascended the home's centrally-located stairs, but soon retreated, running out the door and speaking not a word upon his exit about what terrified him.

As a living museum, the children's bedroom has been resurrected with vintage toys and other period artifacts. These are creepy on their own; however, one old doll looks the worse for wear. It sits on a tiny wooden rocking chair in the corner of the room. Some have seen the doll slowly rocking in the chair all by itself.

Local folklore tells us that one of George and Barbara's sons died by suicide in the upstairs closet. Since the house became a part of the Centre, another door was installed so the closet can be accessed from two bedrooms. Despite the openness this provides, the small space remains the creepiest part of the Oppertshauser House—more on that later in the "Interviews & Firsthand Accounts" section of this book.

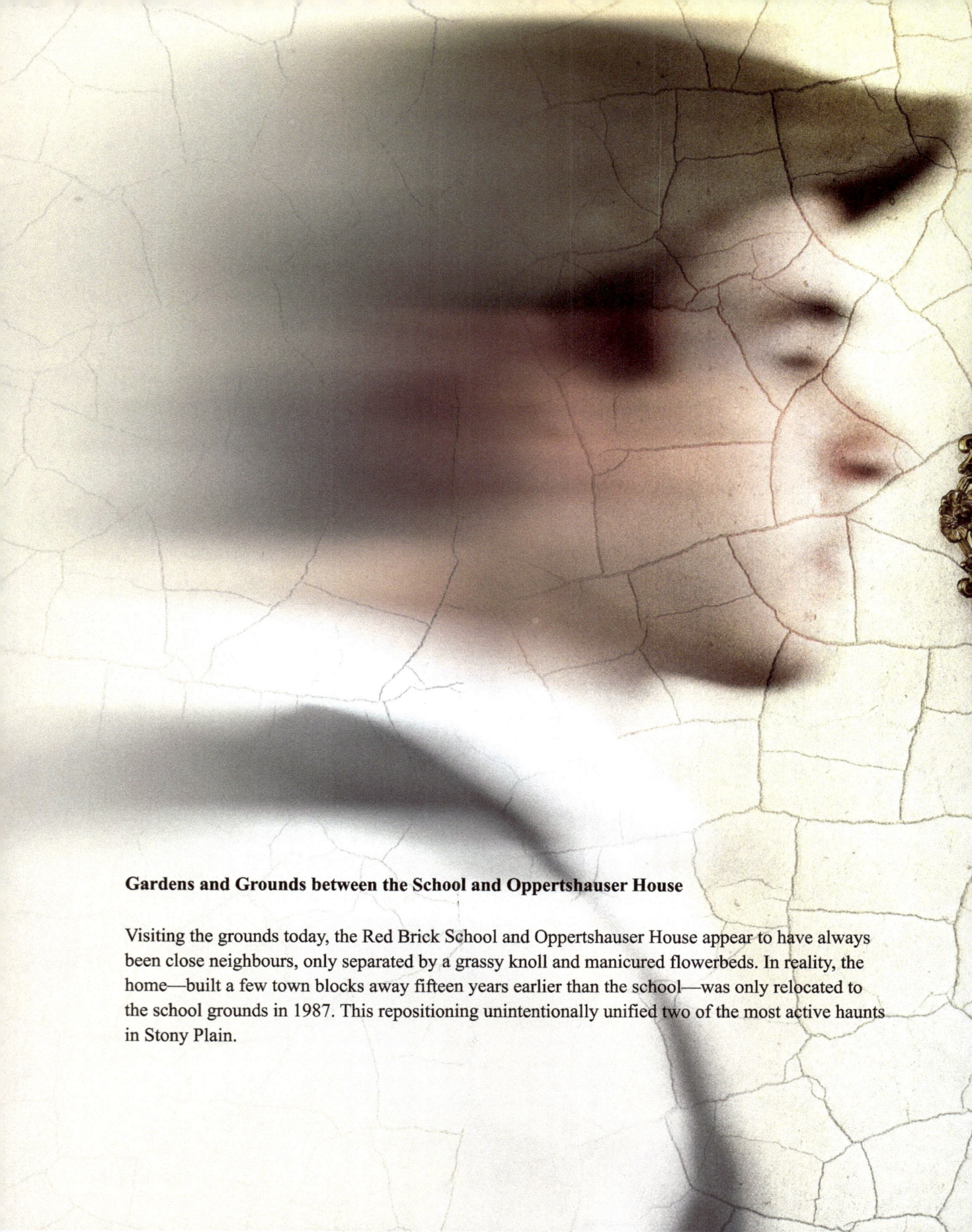

Gardens and Grounds between the School and Oppertshauser House

Visiting the grounds today, the Red Brick School and Oppertshauser House appear to have always been close neighbours, only separated by a grassy knoll and manicured flowerbeds. In reality, the home—built a few town blocks away fifteen years earlier than the school—was only relocated to the school grounds in 1987. This repositioning unintentionally unified two of the most active haunts in Stony Plain.

Debbie Truckey, an employee also interviewed by Barbara Smith for *More Ghost Stories of Alberta*, was locking the south doors of the Red Brick Schoolhouse one summer evening. She turned from the doors to look at the Oppertshauser House and saw a man's face in one window, terrifying her.

The most distinctive feature Debbie reported was his high white collar, reminiscent of men's attire of a bygone era. That is not the only window where ghostly figures have appeared. The children's bedroom window is another hot spot of energy. Multiple people have seen a woman looking out from behind the curtains. Could she be the spirit of Barbara Oppertshauser still mourning her son who died tragically?

Interviews & Firsthand Accounts

It's one thing to read about mythology, folklore, and the supernatural in books, and it's another experience altogether when you hear about strange occurrences from people you know and trust. However, it's a whole new level when you encounter the paranormal yourself.

Some actively seek these brushes with mystical energies, the conversations with deceased relatives, and the unexplainable physical response to what cannot be seen. It's the hair on your arms suddenly standing on end or the abrupt shiver of cold in a warm room.

Others stumble upon the supernatural by accident, or on a fun evening out at a ghost tour at their community historical site.

The following seven interviews and firsthand accounts were collected in 2021. The first four are interviews I conducted in-person with Angela Fetch Muzyka, Sandra Teves, Jody Frechette, and on a Zoom video call with Twyla McGann. The other accounts—Erin Greaves, Victoria Marsh, and Sal K.—were sent to me by email, and I share them here in their own words.

All the interviews and firsthand accounts are either from current or former staff at the Multicultural Heritage Centre, or from individuals who have participated in the Centre's ghost tours over the years.

Interview
Angela Fetch Muzyka

After working at the Multicultural Heritage Centre for a year, Angela Fetch Muzyka agreed to lead the ghost tours, despite the odd incidents that had taken place during that year. For example, at around 9:30pm every night, something would fall in the art gallery, making a loud noise. Working late at the Centre, Angela heard this sound and worried that one of the artworks had slipped off its hook. She would rush into the gallery and stop short when she realized that everything was in its proper place. Even between exhibits, the disturbance persisted. "Sometimes there's nothing to fall in there, and it sounds like something has fallen," Angela added, "It's pretty much like clockwork that every time I've been there that late, that will happen."

The art gallery is in the Red Brick Schoolhouse, but Angela's most unnerving encounters took place elsewhere. "Most of the things that have happened to me have happened in the Oppertshauser House."

To lead the ghost tours, Angela explained, the staff might light a few candles and dim the overhead light fixtures, but nothing else was artificially staged. As a tour facilitator, she shared a collection of spooky stories collected over the years. "No smoke and mirrors," Angela affirmed, "There are no fake noises." The type of story shared, for example, was the instance when someone rearranged the old children's farmyard toy set displayed in the Oppertshauser House. When that person returned to look at it shortly after, the pieces had all moved back to exactly where they had been before.

"For me, every time I've gone into the Oppertshauser House, there's been an experience." Angela spoke of studying the facilitator script and then telling the stories during the tour. She refused to go into the child's bedroom, even when leading a group. "I get a bad vibe."

Between the child's bedroom and middle bedroom is a closet that now has access from both sides. The closet has been an energy center in the house—many peculiar experiences have occurred at that location for both visitors and staff. On Angela's first night leading the tour, she came to the part in the script where she was to share the folklore about the closet. It is lore because there is no historical documentation to confirm what may or may not have happened there many years ago. The story goes that that one of George Oppertshauser's sons took his life by suicide, hanging himself in that upstairs closet.

Angela's first time telling this story on tour was a memorable one. "As I am about to tell the story, it feels like somebody is strangling me. My breath starts to constrict, and I can't seem to tell the story, so much so that one of the participants on the ghost tour says to me: 'Are you all right?' They're thinking that I am having an anxiety attack, or a heart attack, or something. They can't feel what I'm feeling, which is like somebody is trying to stop me from telling this story." Angela gestured to her neck as she said these words, as if trying to remove something binding her. "So, I push out the story as fast as I can, and get out… I book it down the stairs and out of the Oppertshauser House where I get my first really good breath. That's the first time I told that story."

"Somebody follows me out [of the house] because they are concerned that I'm actually having a health incident. When I finally get out there and catch my breath, I'm like, 'No, it felt like somebody had me by the throat and was trying to stop me from talking, to stop me from telling the story.'" A person from the tour turned back to the house and took a photograph. The individual later sent Angela the photo. The picture captured more than a ghostly haze.

"It looked like the profile of a person in the upstairs window, and one in the downstairs front window," Angela recalled. To be specific, a white silhouette in the second-floor bedroom window, and another hazy figure in the main floor sitting room. Angela's response to the photo? She laughed with big eyes and managed to say, "I'm never stepping foot in the Oppertshauser House again!"

That was the first night.

The second night Angela led the ghost tour, she was understandably anxious. She even considered not telling the suicide-closet story. Bravely, she led the tour group upstairs in the Oppertshauser House. Once the entire group gathered on the creaky bedroom floor—no one left below—there was a noise back down on the main floor. They choose to ignore the sound, but odd things began to happen upstairs as well.

In the master bedroom, a grate screwed into the wall suddenly fell off. "They'd just finished redoing the house so they would have been checking all those things to make sure they were properly screwed in," Angela said. "The summer students had just finished going through setting the Oppertshauser House up because we were changing the display from being the General Store to it actually being a tour-able museum." The group later discovered that the grate on the main floor had also fallen from the wall.

When Angela told the suicide-closet story for the second time, she was flooded with uncontrollable emotion. "I start sobbing as though somebody that I loved and held the most dear in my life just died. I'm choking through this story as I'm trying to tell it. Something overtook what was happening at that moment." She again ran from the Oppertshauser House and, as she had the night before, felt immediate relief.

A year later, the Centre again asked Angela to run the ghost tours and she refused. She did relent, however, to teach a new staff member—Twyla McGann—how to facilitate the tours instead. She instructed through example, running the event alongside Twyla.

"So, we run the whole ghost tour and this time we get upstairs, it's earlier in the day than we've done it in the past. Nothing happens upstairs, and when we go downstairs, I exit the building, I don't like to hang out in there. While I'm outside, the record player starts playing inside." When the two women compared notes, they both thought the other had turned on the music. Angela did not turn it on before she left the house. Twyla countered: she and the tour group were still lingering upstairs when they heard the music.

To add to the mystery, only part of the tour heard the gramophone. "Half of us heard the music and half of us didn't," Angela said while scratching her head.

Angela reflected on the history she remembered from working at the Centre. Folktales affirm that the main ghost is George Oppertshauser who roamed between the Red Brick Schoolhouse and his old home, his spirit unsettled as he searches for his son who committed suicide.

"The house has great history except for the suicide death," Angela relented. "The Oppertshausers 'adopted' a lot of the children of the neighbourhood. This was a hangout spot for kids. There were kids they adopted, there were kids they had of their own, they supported other families in their community. It was a family house and they really had lots of people there, were taking care of family and community."

"It's got a great history to it, but it's got a vibe, there are certain rooms that give me a vibe. Even in daylight I won't go into the kid's room. The master bedroom I don't mind so much, the bathroom, all of that, but I won't go into the kid's room even in day—and the night makes it worse. I don't like touching that room." She recalled another event: "We held a party there one night and I'm like 'Okay, I will clean- up but I will not turn out the lights.'"

"I try to forget about the Oppertshauser House, honestly," She said with a laugh.

Angela told me of another event, loosely referred to as The Paranormal Night. "The chef, Kevin, put on a lovely supper in the restaurant. Then a group came and explained ghosts, talking about ghost stories, common things that people experience and attribute to supernatural activity but are in fact rationally explainable."

For example, the chat covered the smell of smoke, how it can be trapped in wooden floorboards, releasing the odour many years later when they expand and contract based on the seasons. "It was really neat because they talked about some of the ways that ghost sightings can be debunked, but they also talked about experiences where there actually have been ghosts. It was a really neat night. A lot of people came out. The art gallery was the presentation space."

After the group entered the art gallery to listen to the presentation, Angela checked the time on her analogue watch. She observed how it had frozen in place, the long and short arms no longer ticking forward. Not thinking much of it, she remarked to her husband, "Damn it, I need a new battery for my watch because it stopped."

It wasn't until after the conclusion of the event, when Angela was packing and cleaning-up for the night that she checked her watch out of habit to see what time it was. She was surprised to see it had restarted. Angela could tell that it had resumed at the time the presentation had ended. "I had to reset the time, but otherwise my watch worked fine after that. It had stopped not during supper, but during the actual presentation itself."

Angela told me the urban legend of the little girl and teacher who died in the schoolhouse when quarantining there during the scarlet fever outbreak. The girl's ghost had been seen or felt in the building, mostly on the lower level of the kitchen and dining room. "The day that we did the paranormal event, the little girl wasn't seen down here—" I was interviewing Angela by the kitchen, "—but, upstairs, when I came to turn the lights on the next day, the Easter eggs [used for the Centre's Easter hunts] were found down the hallway."

The eggs, normally kept in the storage closet, lined the top floor hall. Angela laughed with her co-worker for the prank he pulled on her, but his face wore confusion. He hadn't taken the eggs out of storage. "We think that the little girl—because we were here late that night [for the paranormal event]—was displaced from [the kitchen area] so then went to find a space that didn't have a bunch of people."

Angela worked at the Centre from 2016 to 2018.

Interview
Sandra Teves

It was early 2021. Sandra Teves's first week on the job as Front Desk Administrator initiated her to the spooky side of the Multicultural Heritage Centre. On her desk, beside administrative paperwork and a modern computer, sat a 1913 National Cash Register. Its silver-plated design was embossed with floral decorative elements, and it had circular buttons to input prices. The head of the register featured a rectangular glass enclosure where pointed cards pop up to display stages of the sale, such as dollar amounts or NO SALE.

"I always have it set to NO SALE," Sandra began as she looked at the register out of the corner of her eye, clearly still unnerved from her first week at the desk. "One morning, I came in and it was changed to thirty-five cents. I thought… could someone have come in and done something, because you really have to press hard—" Sandra pushed down on a circular button with her pointer finger, exerting force. The historic machine's bell rang, and the wooden cash drawer popped open at the base. "—in order for it to open, and close." Sandra used her full hand to push the drawer shut. "It was very bizarre. There was no cash missing, nothing was changed in the till at all." Sandra shook her head and shrugged, at a loss for a reasonable explanation.

"Yesterday, I had the fan going and the fan was pointed here," Sandra gestured with her left hand toward her desk, "and yet I heard something *thump*. I turned around and noticed that there were little kids' booties on the floor in the back room." The knitted slippers were in an open storage box and intended for the Centre's artisan shop. "I like to convince myself that it was the fan," Sandra continued, "but the fan was not pointing in that direction. It's just… really odd."

Interview
Twyla McGann

Twyla McGann, Centre employee from 2017 to 2020, began her interview with me by stating that much of the lore cannot be verified. The suicide in the Oppertshauser House is one example. "There is no proven evidence that this actually happened because they didn't keep records like that —that were accessible anyway." Twyla spoke of another case in which the upstairs of the schoolhouse was used as an infirmary during a particularly bad flu season and multiple people died. "There is no mention of that in the old *Star*, the old newspapers, but you just didn't report on stuff like that. The flu used to be deadly."

Twyla often heard unusual noises when standing in the art gallery in the Red Brick Schoolhouse. "It doesn't matter the time of day or the time of year." She would pause to listen. Even when the grounds were empty, she could hear murmured talking, as if people were in conversation in another part of the building. Twyla couldn't make out what was said, but she was certain that one of the voices was male. Once, she even experienced this with others.

Twyla was working in the art gallery one summer day. "Two restaurant staff came upstairs. I'm standing with them when we all hear this mumbled talking [coming from the kitchen on the floor below]. And I'm like, 'Oh, Lynn [the cook] must be getting a delivery,' because it was actually quite a boisterous voice. You could really hear it."

Twyla parted ways with the restaurant staff. "They went downstairs, I went about tidying up the gallery." It was only a few moments later before they raced back upstairs to inform Twyla that no one was in the kitchen. "Lynn wasn't there. There was no delivery person there. There was nothing that could confirm that voice." Yet, they all had heard the boisterous man's speech coming from the floor below.

"Working [at the Centre], there was always weird stuff, thumps and bumps and noises and odd things. But the most phenomenal stuff, the stuff that makes me think still today, 'oh that was really, really cool,' always happened during the ghost tours. The atmosphere was right. The energy was right or something for these things to happen."

Twyla shared that one special aspect of the ghost tours was that people could have shared experiences. Two people could feel, sense, or see the same thing. There have also been incidents where only part of a group would have a particular spooky encounter.

"We would occasionally bring out toys for the ghost tours. One of these was an EMF reader that is supposed to pick up on the energy of spiritual activity. During a ghost tour we were using the EMF reader and recording, and we did get some readings upstairs by the refrigerator in the log cabin that would suggest, in one particular spot, that there was an energy. About three and a half feet [tall] and only in this spot, and only that evening. It never happened again."

Twyla then led that group down the stairs to the lower level where she began telling the story of the janitor who, alone in the building, mopped the hallway only to discover snowy footprints a moment later. "I pointed the EMF reader right at the spot that I was talking about with these snowy footprints and it went crazy! And the ghost tour participants went crazy! And it never happened again."

Twyla reflected about the ghost-hunting tool: "The cool thing about these little devices, whether or not you want to believe in them, they do have neat things that can happen on their own and you can't get it to repeat it, so it's not as cut and dry as you'd think. Like, if it went off the first time because an air conditioner was on for some reason and it caused it to go off, we couldn't recreate it at any point in time."

What I gathered from Twyla's reflection was that the EMF readings were bizarre. Were they simply coincidences? Was the reader triggered by the air conditioner or a ghost tour participant's cell phone? Perhaps. That would be the rational conclusion. However, the fact that the EMF device went berserk at two exact spots where others had reported a child-ghost in the Cabin and the mysterious footprints in the basement hall does raise an important question. Exactly how many corroborated accounts must there be before we accept the notion that something is going on beyond what we can easily explain?

"We were doing spirit box recordings," Twyla continued. She was using an app on her smart phone. (More on spirit boxes in the "Paranormal Investigation" section.) "The idea is that it cycles through radio signals at a fast pace in an effort to allow anyone or anything who wants to communicate an opportunity to manipulate the sounds." Twyla was leading a large ghost tour hired by a company as an employee team-building exercise. They were in the lower level of the schoolhouse, in the additional seating gallery of the restaurant. Twyla typically began by asking if a spirit was with them in the room. She felt suddenly compelled to ask a different question. "Did you come here with someone tonight?" she said.

The response from the spirit box was, "Yes," so she probed further. Twyla asked who the ghost had come with that night. The response was, "David." Sure enough, there was a David in the group. "David went wild," Twyla said as she thought back to that night. "And his co-workers went wild."

"I don't know the goings on of the spirit world," she reflected of her urge to ask the question that night. Twyla has had many spooky experiences using the spirit box; however, she doesn't discount the possibility of coincidence. Her attitude seems to be one of openness to the possibility of an encounter and a focus on fun as a part of the tour experience.

Twyla saved the best story for last—which she firmly stated is unmanipulated or sensationalized in any way. "This is my very first ghost tour. Angela had done the ghost tours in the past and because it was my first year I didn't know what the heck I was doing. She offered to come and give the ghost tour, and then I could watch, but the problem was that she had a bad experience on her last ghost tour and didn't feel comfortable hanging out in the Oppertshauser House for very long."

"We went through the ghost tour in the Oppertshauser House, and we were suddenly all upstairs and Angela talks about the last story. We're supposed to give an opportunity [for the participants] to walk around with their cameras and gather evidence." Angela told Twyla she would wait outside and left. The group milled about, snapping photos and exploring the bedrooms. Twyla was using the spirit box app.

"I was getting some weird things happening on my phone, so I was sharing it with a crowd of people in the little hallway. It is really cramped up there so you can imagine twelve to twenty people up there. I'm in the hallway with five or six other ladies and one gentleman and we hear music and chatter coming from the living room. We all looked in the direction of the stairs and I said out loud, 'Oh, Angela must be playing the phonograph for another guest.' It was clearly music and party chatter as if there was a cocktail party downstairs."

"We wrapped up just a few minutes later and go downstairs and the living room is completely empty. All the guests were upstairs with me. As we made our way outside, Angela was there on the deck. I said, 'Were you inside at all? Did you play the phonograph?'"

Angela responded: "Nope, not at all."

The ghost tour participants who heard the music and chatter with Twyla that day return to the Centre every year. They are eager to encounter the supernatural again. "It was pretty phenomenal," Twyla said. "It was pretty neat—and mostly because more than one person experienced it."

Twyla affirmed that she does not believe in ghosts.

"I do [believe, however]," she added with a chuckle, "when I'm giving ghost tours."

Interview
Jodi Frechette

"We've had tons of experiences since day one," Jodi Frechette said when I asked if she'd had any spooky encounters while running her business, Wheet Nothings Gluten Free Diner, in the kitchen at the Multicultural Heritage Centre. They started work on the space in April 2021.

"We've done a lot of renovations in the place, which is notorious for stirring up spirits. The first two weeks that we were in here, my fiancé Kevin was renovating in the dining room down the hall, and I was sitting here with my laptop filling out numerous forms. We were the only two people in the building. He came down after a couple of hours of working and I said, 'Things have already started.' He said, 'What are you talking about?' I could hear kids running around in the gymnasium upstairs, like they were in gym class. It would stop every once in a while, and then you could hear distinct footsteps running across the floor."

One spring morning, Jodi and Kevin arrived bright and early. They turned off the alarm and set down their groceries for the restaurant in the kitchen. Jodi noticed something unusual. She left the kitchen and approached Kevin, who had resumed construction of the front counter, and said, "Kev, come here for a second." She led him into the kitchen, then pointed.

"Did you take that vent out yesterday?" she asked. He said no and supposed it might have fallen out of the ceiling. If it had simply dropped, the metal might have been dented—plus, Jodi noticed, the vent cover was laying on the ground two feet away from the open hole, not directly under the opening.

Shortly after Kevin went back to work building the counter, Jodi came out to talk to him. She stopped dead in her tracks. He said, "What?" but she simply pointed past him. "Did you turn the fireplace on?" she asked.

He replied, "I don't know how to turn the fireplace on."

There was a manual power switch on the back of the fireplace. The couple wondered if they forgot to turn off the fire the night before. If they had, however, the fan mounted to the top of the cast-iron

fireplace would have been spinning. The fan is fed by heat: the hotter it gets, the faster it spins. The fan was not triggered that morning. Nor was the metal hot when Kevin touched it.

Another morning, Kevin entered the building first, before Jodi and her son. He needed to collect his tools that he had left in the dining room at the far end of the hall from the kitchen. No one had been in the Centre over the weekend and Jodi and Kevin had locked up. The place was quiet. As Kevin approached the dining gallery, all the hairs on the back of his neck and arms begin to stand on end. He opened the dining room doors and heard the sound of static. Supposing it was the radio, he went to turn it off, but it was not plugged in. Then he noticed that the sink in the room, which no one ever used, was turned on full blast.

After another full day of renovating, Jodi and Kevin were at the Centre late at night. A few of their friends had stopped by to do a tour of the place and have a little visit. They were sitting at one of the tables near the kitchen, talking and having a few drinks. The radio played quietly in the background. There were a couple of extra chairs sitting in the hall that they had moved out of the dinning gallery that day while working.

One of their friends, Arthur, rose from the table, passed through the hall, and entered the bathroom. When he returned to the table, he asked the group, "Which one of you put a chair in the men's bathroom."

Jodi likely scrunched her brow then, as she did now in retelling the story to me. "Nobody. We've all been sitting here the whole time, Arthur," she told him. Jodi and her friend Shawn went to investigate. Sure enough, there was a chair pushed up against the wall inside the men's washroom. Shawn carried the chair back into the hall. "That was kinda weird," they agreed as a group.

It was beginning to get late and dark outside, so the friends decided to tour the Red Brick Schoolhouse before parting for the evening. There were two staircases leading from the kitchen level to a landing, before a single stairway ascended to the main floor of the building. The stairs on the left had one door and narrow steps. On the right, there were double doors and a wide stairway. "We went up the single door access and did a tour all through the top." Jodi was using a spirit box app. "I have a white noise app on my phone," said Jodi, "because [ghosts] can take energy from it, and they get stronger when they have an energy source." While walking around, Jodi said, "If there's anybody here, can you move that chair again so we know you're here?"

This time, they descended to the lower level by the wider stairs and entered the hall through the double doors. Jodi was the first one to reach the hallway and she turned to the right. "I just stopped. I looked at everybody and said, 'Did any of you come downstairs while we were upstairs?'" Kevin and their friends responded "No," they had all stuck together.

"That chair that had been up against the wall was now pushed up with its back completely against that door that we had gone up. If we had come back down that way, when we opened that door, the chair would have been right there."

On a car ride home from the Centre one night, Jodi reflected on their experience. It was not the first time she'd heard of chairs moving seemingly on their own. She recalled the story of a former director who encountered stacked chairs pushed up against the wall of the dining gallery, though no one could figure out who had done it.

"I said to Kevin, 'You know what? I think I know what it is. I think I know why those chairs are moving. Remember in [the Cabin] they had the rules of the classroom from the 1920's? One of the rules is that students have to take their chairs and push them against the wall every day at the end of the day so the teacher can sweep.'"

Alberta Education

Jodi was referring to a document on display in the Pioneer Cabin on the noticeboard of community news. The source was unknown, but the document began by listing the "Rules for Teachers" in 1915. These instructions included when marriage was permissible—not during the term of your contract—evening curfew, wardrobe—no bright colours—and the final rule of keeping the school room neat and clean. There was a similar, "Rules for Students," however it was undated. The tenth rule stated, "If the master calls your name after class, straighten the benches and tables. Sweep the room, dust, and leave everything tidy."

"The creepiest [story] wasn't even us," Jodi continued, not missing a beat. "Our granddaughter is three[-years-old] and she came with her mom one day to visit us because they lived just down the street. She walked in and she kept saying, 'Grandma, where are my bunk beds?'" Jodi told her granddaughter that her bed was at Grandma's and Grandpa's house, but her granddaughter didn't believe her. She insisted on going upstairs to look for herself. As soon as they reached the main floor where the front desk was located, the child said, "Shh, Grandma, be quiet. There are monsters in here." Jodi told me how intuitive her grandchild was, also sensing a ghost in the basement of their family home.

Jodi took her granddaughter to tour the top floor of the schoolhouse. Again, when the child returned to the main level, she sensed something odd. Before she set foot on the wooden floor from the stairway, she turned back to the adults behind her and said, "Grandma, there are ghosts in here."

There is something unnerving about children experiencing the paranormal. Jodi and her family felt this that day. "The heebie-jeebies" she called it. That wasn't the end of it either!

The family headed into the Cabin to look around at the old stove, tools, school desk, and other artifacts. Jodi's granddaughter asked if she could play with the old toys and dolls. At the foot of the pioneer bed stood a shin-high wooden cradle with blankets and baby dolls. The dolls were worn, their paint chipping and wirehair tangled. They looked well loved in a previous life. Jodi's granddaughter picked up the first baby and rocked it, smoothed its hair. She replaced it in the cradle and reached for another.

"She pulled her hand back," Jodi recalled, "and looked at me, and said, 'Grandma, I don't like that baby.'" Her granddaughter then wanted out of the Cabin immediately, eager to return to the kitchen.

The final story Jodi shared with me was another bizarre event in the kitchen. "This one was super weird," she began. "Between the kitchen and dish pit area, there are two hanging wire shelves that have click-in metal brackets. You have to lift them up and then click them down. The day before we were opening [to the public], we were here all day cooking. My fiancé was in the dish pit, running

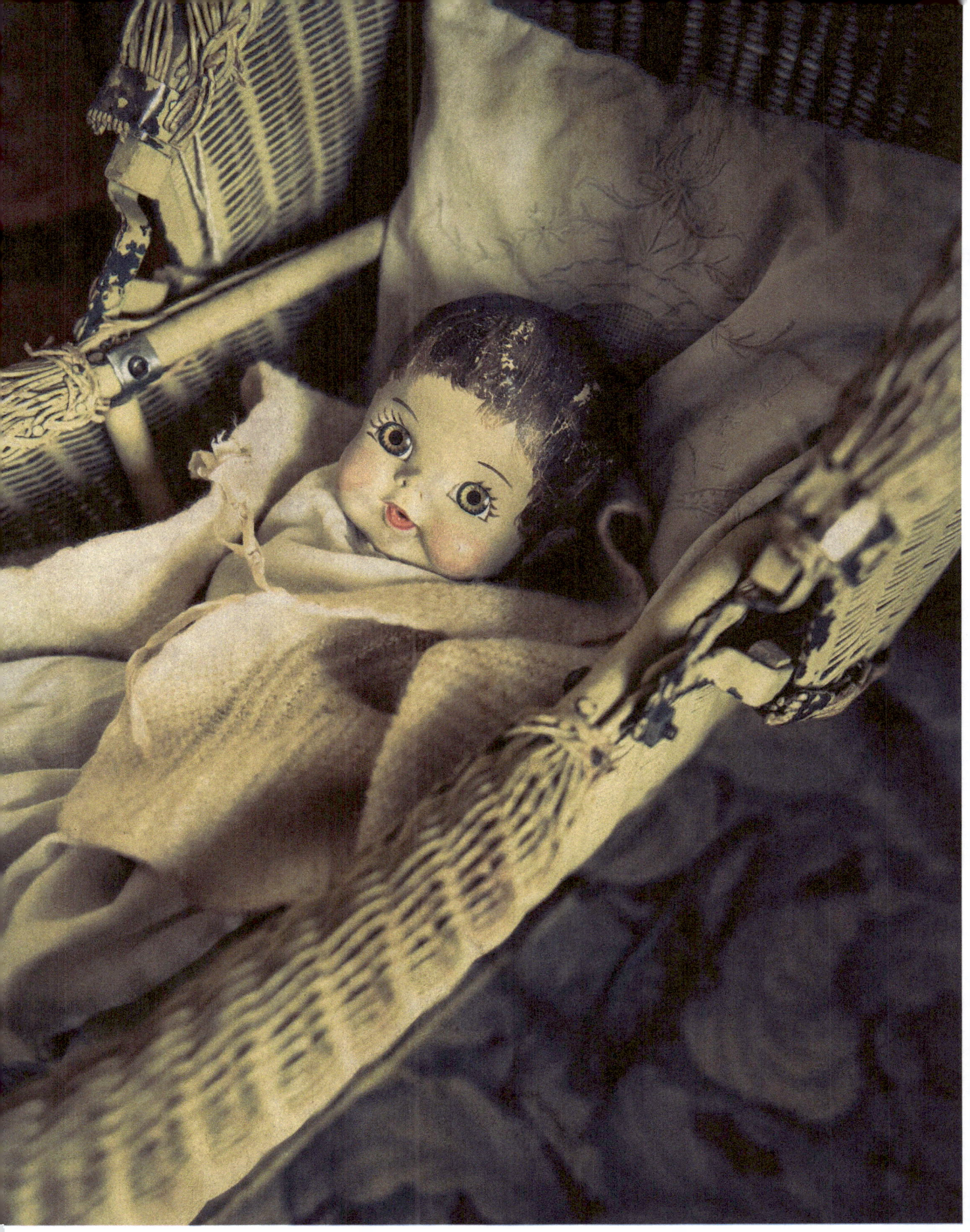

dishes; my son was prepping all the vegetables for the next day; and I was busy cooking and pulling [baking] out of the oven to slice."

"I was walking around the corner from the ovens and just as I got to the entrance, I turned my head and one of those brackets came flying straight out from the wall and hit the floor. I was like, 'What just happened?' I set the [baking] down. We all heard it. It was metal so it hit the floor and clanged. We all turned around and looked at that shelf and it was sitting there hovering —with only one bracket on one side. We were all looking at it and we looked at each other, and as soon as we looked away, that shelf went flying down and smashed everything."

Jodi was mystified. "Those brackets have to be physically picked up and pulled out."

Firsthand Account Erin Greaves

"My story comes from a Halloween tour my husband and I did on October 28, 2017. I apologize, I don't remember the guide's name, but I believe she was fairly new at the time and was very friendly.

"We arrived at the main brick building early and were told we could look around a bit until everyone entered. I believe our group was about ten people or so in total.

"While we were waiting for the last few people to arrive, we started exploring the Centre, never having been there before, and ended up upstairs in the museum reading the different displays. I felt pulled towards a display showing off Cornelia Wood's hats and made the comment to my husband, 'Look at all her hats, those are so neat.'

"We went back downstairs to join the group and started the official Halloween tour. The first spot we went was upstairs again to view the museum. My husband and I had been the last ones up there and the first ones to go back up after the tour guide. As soon as we got upstairs, I noticed the cupboard underneath Cornelia's display was wide open and showed off a bunch more of Cornelia's hats that were stored instead of displayed. It may have just been a coincidence, but it felt to me like Cornelia was trying to show off the rest of her hat collection after I made the comment about how neat I thought her hats were."

Cornelia Wood hat collection. Lower cabinet ajar.
Photo credit Erin Greaves

"Our second experience that night was when we went into the Oppertshauser House with the rest of the group. As soon as we stepped in, we had an eerie feeling of being watched. We chalked that up to the Halloween atmosphere and how spooky that night felt overall. We all gathered in the dining room area to listen to the guide tell us more about the family and, suddenly, we heard a *BANG*, like something big had just fallen over. The sound came from upstairs, almost right above us.

"The guide stopped and looked a bit worried and asked if anyone in our group had gone upstairs already without waiting. A couple of people closer to the living room—also closest to the stairs—said no, there was no one that went up there ahead of them. We all kind of ignored [the sound] and finished listening to the guide's stories and then headed as a group upstairs. Sure enough, no one had been up there ahead of us. It was empty until our group got up there and we would have heard if anyone had been there as the floors were so creaky.

"We explored upstairs as a group, looking at the bedrooms, and for anything that could have possibly fallen—nothing looked obvious to any of us—and then gathered again to listen to the stories. Suddenly, the guide started getting very emotional and kept grabbing at her throat as she was telling us about one of the family members who had hung himself in the closet that adjoined two of the bedrooms. She said it also felt that way the night before when she was giving the tour, and she got such a bad feeling when she'd talk about it.

"Thinking of it afterwards, the bang we had heard could almost have been the sound of a stool or chair being kicked out from someone who had hung themselves. Sure enough, the closet was pretty much directly over us when we were all standing downstairs as a group.

"I know there is a photo from a member of the tour that night… The photo is from when the tour was over, and we were all walking back to our cars. [A person] took a photo of the Oppertshauser House and it looks to me like three spirits are looking back out at us. I believe there were two down in the living room area and one upstairs [looking out] from one of the bedroom windows."

Photo supplied by Erin Greaves taken by another unknown participant of the same ghost tour.

Firsthand Account Victoria Marsh

"I worked in the Oppertshauser House from summer to Christmas in 2016, solely on weekends as I worked full-time [elsewhere]. At this time, the House was a general store, selling items made by local artisans, along with candy and local-interest books.

"For some context, I come from a family that has indeed experienced paranormal phenomena—both my parents have had intuitive flashes, including dreams and tangible reactions to events that had not happened yet. One [of those incidents] included my mother feeling a car accident-like impact. A week later, I was hit head-on and she actually found me on a road she didn't normally take.

"While I've had some intuitive experiences, I seem to only notice objects being moved. In my old apartment where I lived alone, little sauce bowls would be flipped over in the drying rack, my Xbox was disconnected at the adapter beneath my TV cabinet, and I've watched my Amazon remote rock back and forth after hearing it being dropped on the coffee table—even though it had been lying there flat and I was across the room, alone.

"The first experience I had at the Oppertshauser House was with a stone carving that was sitting on a tall wood cabinet with open shelving. It was a smaller sculpture, maybe three to four inches in height, and had a stable base to it. I was alone in the house and it was toward the end of the day, so I was going through the house to tidy up and get all the makers' displays reset and ready for the next day.

"I wasn't looking at the shelving unit, I believe I was on the other side of the living room, but I heard something. I turned and could see one of the sculptures rocking back and forth, very much as if someone had bumped the cabinet. There were several pieces on the same shelf, and more items on the cabinet as a whole, but only one item was rocking. I tried to replicate the motion by stomping and stepping heavy, in case I had done something, but nothing moved that cabinet or items, not even jumping up and down in front of it.

"The second event, I was in the house alone again, probably at around 2pm or so. The upstairs bedrooms were used as offices at the time. There were sometimes staff in on Saturday mornings

An orb of light above the railing leading to the bedroom floor of the Oppertshauser House. Photo provided by Victoria Marsh which she took in 2018 during the October ghost tours in the Oppertshauser house. Unedited photo, captured with an iPhone 5S.

catching up, but they would always let me know when they were gone so that I could turn on the alarms once we had closed for the day. I believe it was a Sunday in late summer with not great weather—so we hadn't had many customers come through at all. I was in the porch area, where the till was, and suddenly I heard music blasting from upstairs. Even when we would have staff working up there, I never really heard them, so this was very unusual.

"I thought maybe someone had come back, so I called upstairs, but there was no one. I tried to never leave the store area unattended, in case of theft, but I popped upstairs, and someone's locked computer was playing music loudly. I simply turned the volume down on the speakers and walked out.

"The only other situation [I had in the Oppertshauser House] was the basement light turning off when I walked by the staircase on the main floor. I was making my rounds through the house—again, alone—and as I'm walking by, a light in the basement turns off.

"I rushed out to the back deck to see if someone had exited through the basement door, but there was no one. I'm not sure what the basement is used for now, but back then it was storage and had the staff washroom. To keep customers from wandering around the [basement of the] house, the light was kept off, so this was strange."

Firsthand Account
Sal K.

"There were three separate experiences during the tour. The first two, I tried to find rational explanations for, but the last one I couldn't. I'd like to preface by saying that I have been on several ghost tours—mainly in Edmonton—and have been to some very creepy places with some dark history. I even worked in a haunted cabin (voluntarily) for a year at Jasper Park Lodge. I don't rattle easily. I can honestly say that the energy and overall feeling at the Multicultural Heritage Centre and the Oppertshauser House was very different, and it actually made me nervous.

"The tour started in the main Centre and as far as I understood, the tour guide was the only one working on the grounds that evening. As our group left the Centre to tour the Oppertshauser House, we exited by the backdoor and I set my drink down on a surface with the intention of retrieving it on the way back. The tour guide locked the doors and the group moved over to the house. When we came back, my drink was gone. Not overly paranormal and possibly could be explained. Maybe another worker arrived and disposed of it or someone from the group threw it out?

"The second experience was in the Oppertshauser House. The group was upstairs and spread out through the bedrooms and hallway as the guide was telling us the history and some stories. Everyone was quiet and listening when a heavy iron wall grate fell out of the wall and onto the floor, scaring the shit out of everyone. It was right next to me behind a door. This could also have been explained by someone possibly bumping into the wall on the other side of it or perhaps the door was opened too far, hitting the wall and it popped out?

"The third experience happened when the group left the house to go back to the [Red Brick Schoolhouse]. We all exited, the tour guide made sure everyone left and that all the lights were shut off on the way out. She locked the door and we started to make our way to the [school] when someone looked back and announced that the top floor lights were all on. Even the tour guide was a little freaked out as we stared at the lights, wondering how they had all turned on again. The guide ended the tour by stating that when we leave, to make sure that we are respectful, thank the ghosts for the opportunity to explore, but to make sure that we ask them to stay behind and not travel home with us. After that last experience, I definitely took her advice!"

Paranormal Investigations

From what I've learned, paranormal investigations take place just as often to discount the presence of spirits as to confirm their existence. It's a process of asking probing questions. Did we see a luminous woman at the window? Or did our brain organize the patterns and shapes we perceived into a recognisable human form? Perhaps the conversation at the spooky setting prompted us to manifest what we saw?

Are the footsteps and door creeks caused by a visiting spook? Or are these infrasounds—low frequency noises—vibrations that our minds translate into auditory phenomena? What we heard and felt may be from a nearby construction site, or even disturbances in air pressure from thunderstorms.

These are the types of questions asked by paranormal investigators. They record data in a variety of ways and open themselves to the energy of the location in question. With curiosity, they explore. Their goal is to understand the history and disturbances of each location. They review the footage gathered on the scene and ask themselves if the paranormal activity can be explained in a logical way.

A former Centre employee recommended an illuminating Ted Talk featuring Carrie Poppy. In the video from TEDxVienna, filmed in October 2016, Carrie talks about her own personal haunting at a guest house where she resided for a time.

Carrie sensed that she was being watched. No one was there, only her two dog companions. She felt a heavy pressure on her chest. She also heard a sound like wind, a whoosh that would pass right through her. On the advice of a friend, she did a cleansing ritual with burning sage, hoping to rid the space of the spooky presence. Nothing changed, the ghost remained, along with the foreboding feelings and intense chest pains.

Carrie began to research hauntings online. She discovered a group of ghost-debunkers whose mission was to find scientific explanations for paranormal encounters. They told her to consider carbon monoxide poisoning. She did some reading and sure enough, the symptoms of her haunting were identical to a person residing in a dwelling with a gas leak. She called the gas company

immediately and upon their inspection learned that she might not have survived the night. They detected extremely high levels of carbon monoxide in the guest house.

Carrie is now a paranormal investigator herself. With a big smile, she proclaimed, "Nine times out of ten, science wins, it saves the day, it's all explained—but that's not true. The truth is: ten times out of ten, science wins."

She went on to explain that there are two types of truth, from her perspective. "Outer truth and inner truth." Outer truth is what we can historically or scientifically verify: what observably happened that can't be refuted. Inner truth, on the other hand, comes down to our personal experiences, beliefs, and values. This allows room for mystery to exist, those things we cannot explain. Carrie told the audience that she still hoped to encounter a ghost on one of her investigations. In the meantime, she advocated for us all to show respect to one other, no matter what we individually believe.

Ghost Hunting Tools

EMF Meter

The EMF meter, sometimes referred to as a K-II meter, senses electromagnetic fields, EMF, and displays their strength on the remote-sized, battery-powered device. LED lights illuminate from green to red indicating normal to extremely high electromotive force field, typically ranging from 1.5 mG (milliGAUSS) to 20+ mG. The meter's intended purpose was to detect high radiation from appliances like microwaves, refrigerators, computers, and printers, but ghost hunters have adopted the technology. Prices online range from $30 to $300 CAD.

Infrared Camera

A specialized infrared camera allows ghost hunters to investigate a location with the lights off. The infrared capabilities record in black and white, allowing the recording to capture details in extremely low light situations. Prices online range from $350 to $2,000.

Audio Recorder

As many apparitions choose not to manifest themselves visually, an audio recorder can capture voices and other unusual noises. The recordings may detect sounds at ultra-low or ultra-high frequencies beyond the range of human hearing, which can then be replayed later and examined. Prices online range from $30 to $400.

Spirit Box

A Spirit Box, sometimes called a Ghost Box, is a battery powered tool that scans AM and FM radio waves. Some Spirit Boxes also detect temperature. Ghost hunters use this device to listen for communicating spirits who will draw out words from the white noise. Prices online range from $160 to $300.

You can also download Spirit and Ghost Box apps onto your phone. These work by allowing access to a "voice bank", which consists of short pieces of speech that can be combined by the spirit to form full words and messages. Prices for the apps range from free to $30 subscriptions.

Investigation ParanorBill

Bill Connelly, also known as ParanorBill, is an Edmonton-based paranormal investigator. A fifth-generation undertaker, Bill has experienced the supernatural from childhood and has devoted himself to focused research and investigation for more than twenty years. In his investigation reports, he shares that every culture and religion has their own beliefs about life after death. His mission is to understand and connect with the other side. These are the perspectives that informed Bill's visit to the Multicultural Heritage Centre in 2009 with his small team, ready to explore the reports of otherworldly activity. He shared his findings in three videos on his YouTube channel (Bill ParanorBill Connelly) on September 9, 2009.

Bill interviewed Marge Proctor, the manager of the artisan market and gift shop that was located on the main floor of the Oppertshauser House at that time. "I sell little motion sensors, birds and frogs that chirp and tweet," she began. "I was working at my till area by the computer and those things were going crazy in another room. I was the only one in here. The doors were locked, there was no activity. We have no pets that live in the house." Nothing could account for why the motion sensors went off that day. She also shared that she smelled pipe tobacco on numerous occasions.

"I saw my first apparition just before Christmas," Marge continued. "Again, I was alone. It was around four o'clock and I was getting ready to close the store. I was coming to do a walkthrough to make sure there were no people left in the store because I wanted to close up. I saw the side of a woman's head. She was in another room… I started to speak to her and ask her if she needed help with anything. By the time I got through the doorway she had vanished. I walked around the whole store looking for her, but it was just me." She added that the woman was blonde with her hair pulled back on one side.

Marge told another story about hanging artwork in the Oppertshauser House. The ladder, of its own volition, began to wobble back and forth. She yelled at George, "Cut it out, quit it!" The ladder became immediately still.

On interview day, Bill Connolly took a preliminary video walking up the home's creaky staircase and inadvertently recorded the sound of whistling. He had not heard the noise at the time, but that is a common occurrence. In many paranormal investigations, disembodied sounds and voices (called electronic voice phenomena, or EVP) are only audible through recording devices, which is why reviewing all footage is an essential part of the process.

The video then switches gears from the interview to Bill and his team setting up their equipment after dark. Imagine a high-tech surveillance system that includes:
- 3 digital voice recorders
- 2 high-definition video recorders
- 4 high resolution night vision cameras
- A 16-channel digital video recorder
- 3 K-II Meters
- 3 Mel-8704R Meters
- 1 computer and monitor

On the bedroom level of the Oppertshauser House, one team member asked, "George, are you here with me?" Recorder #2 picked up a response. The audio was enhanced after the fact, and the researchers confirmed the answer: "YES... Bill."

In the second of the three ParanorBill videos, one of the researchers sensed a presence. Recorder #3 in the living room picked up a disembodied voice that said, "Stay out." Bill noticed a temperature drop. Reviewing the video recording, they saw a floating orb. Bill gave a definition of an orb, stating:

The Orb Theory
The "Orb" is the energy being used or taken from any energy source a Spirit has available to it. Using this Energy, the Spirit can manifest itself.

Footage from Infrared Camera #4 at 12:47 AM framed a view of the main floor of the Oppertshauser House in its General Store iteration. In the video, we see a rack of greeting cards, a lamp, art on the walls, and a display of fabrics. Initially, the scene appeared fixed, unmoving apart from a speck of dust that wafted through the space. Even in the enhanced and zoomed-in footage, viewers might struggle to see the "orb" until we come to understand that what appeared to be a speck of dust, which looks loonie-sized and hazy-white in the video, is in fact the ghostly presence that ParanorBill picked-up on.

Then, the camera began to shake, but not the kind of jiggle when a handheld recording device moved due to human fatigue. The footage indicated that the camera jerked slightly up and down, as if nodding. Now that we viewers know what to look for, we spot the second occurrence of the orb of light flitting through the General Store.

The video switches to a view of an electromagnetic radiation tester in cameraman-technician Charles Sigouin's hand as he walks slowly through the house. He was simultaneously filming what he saw. We hear faint beeps and then a voice, followed by a click. "What the hell was that?" Charles asked. "That was a phone, like an answering machine or somethin'—but it was like it was on speakerphone."

Todd McLean, a fellow investigator in the living room, responded, "I don't know man, I just got the weirdest feeling like I was gonna fill my pants."

The video cuts to Charles, who addressed the viewer about the voice he and his colleague heard. They enhanced the audio recording and reported that the female apparition said, "It's just me playing with Phone."

Bill confirmed who had been in the house at the time: a female staff member who had fallen asleep; a male cook in the basement; and himself, Charles, and Todd. He reflected that the voice they heard in the recording was not the same as the sleeping woman's. He ruled her out. He also wondered at the oddity of what was said, that the voice didn't say she was playing with *the* phone or even *testing* the phone. The recording was, "It's just me playing with Phone."

In the comments below the video, a person asked how the investigators were able to get such a clear recording of the voice. Bill replied in the comments, writing, "It was left on the answering machine & we had a Digital Recorder set up there as there have been reports of voices in that room. Funny thing is the phone didn't ring, it just beeped and there was the voice."

Investigation
The Alberta Paranormal Investigators Society

Beth Fowler assembled a team and began investigating the paranormal as far back as 2004. With the desire to provide regulation for their industry, they formed The Alberta Paranormal Investigators Society Inc. as a not-for-profit in 2009. They implemented a code of ethics and bylaws, running background checks on initiating members.

Their mandate was to use the scientific method to research potential haunts. They gathered information through quantifiable data, such as video and audio recordings, photography, and other environmental evidence. They did not rely on spiritualist readings, such as the work of mediums or psychics, as they believed that these were not as reliable and had the reputation of profiteering from and misleading homeowners worried about spirits.

The Society became inactive in 2013, and the poor health of its founder, Beth, continued its unravelling. As of the current update on the Society's website, which I read in autumn 2021, Beth hoped to form a new team in 2019, however there is no indication to suggest this took place. The Society's YouTube channel and Facebook page, however, have been maintained and are up to date.

The Paranormal Investigators Society of Alberta conducted two investigations at the Multicultural Heritage Centre. One took place on October 26, 2012. Videos with footage from these explorations, recorded on Hi8 Sony tape, can be found on their YouTube channel (TheAlbertaParanormal). The investigation team that conducted the research included:
- Beth, Society President, Head Investigator
- Brian N., Vice President
- Brenda, Lead Investigator
- Jess, Investigator

The team executed baseline tests with their equipment to record and establish the normal EMF levels given off in the space from computers and monitors, printers, phones, and lights. They found no abnormal EMF readings. Brenda and Beth went on to do an electronic voice phenomenon experiment in the Oppertshauser House closet where the suicide allegedly took place. Just as they were setting up their experiment, one of the overhead lights went out. They played an audio recording of a woman's voice, set to the same frequency as the recording they would be capturing.

Their recording said, "Are you here? If you can hear us, please make a noise." The pre-recorded voice continued, telling the possible ghosts that the investigators were there in respect for the dead, with the sole desire of communication and offering condolences. The voice was soothing, therapy-like with the aim of instilling comfort and encouraging a response. None was given.

The Society's second experiment took place in the upstairs bedroom using an old-fashioned method more common prior to the invention of spirit boxes. They turned on a radio frequency and recorded the white noise. One of the investigators held the camera while another asked questions, such as, "Is George here?" Nothing elicited a response.

They decided to turn off the white noise and began using an EMF reader, asking more questions, and watching the lights barely flicker. They both heard a sound. Something airy and indistinct. One woman asked the other if it was her stomach, and she replied that it wasn't.

The investigator using the EMF reader demonstrated that a human could not set off the device by passing her hand in front of it. Suddenly, all the lights illuminated in the darkened room. The investigators thanked the spirit for making its presence known. They asked about the identity of the spirit, suggesting names and waiting for a reply. To the name 'George,' the lights flashed vigorously, and the same response came when they inquired if George enjoyed scaring a man on the stairs the other day.

The woman verbally sympathised with George, affirming that the house was his, that the visiting man needed to respect that. The investigators continued to interact with the presence, talking about how George and his family were German. The lights continued to flash. The women commented on how amazing their "hits" were, stating that they hadn't experienced that much paranormal activity since their investigation at CKUA, an Edmonton radio station.

They conducted further experiments in the Oppertshauser House living room, set-up at that time with shelves and wares for sale in the General Store. One investigator sang an old German song, "Du du liegst mir im herzen," translated to "You, you are in my heart." The audio replay suggested they could hear a mysterious voice repeating, "Du, du," from the song.

Other experiments record a variety of phenomena to be reviewed later for sounds such as a noise that might have been a name spoken faintly while one investigator walked up the stairs. Jess began using a spirit box, though Beth was skeptical. She felt those devices and apps were susceptible to

the psychological responses of those using them. Still, the recording of that experiment yielded results she found interesting. She deciphered multiple German words, and other English words like, "Get out," "Don't like," and, "Annoying."

They asked the spirit to identify itself. They heard a random swash of words amidst the radio waves. "Just get out," for example, and "Please go away." One recording suggested they were talking to a ghost named Elizabeth.

Brenda and Beth left the Oppertshauser House and went into the Pioneer Cabin at the Red Brick School. Brenda recalled her handheld recorder turning off by itself in the Cabin during a previous investigation, despite having 45 minutes of recording time left in the battery. It had also zoomed in on Brian all by itself, then failed to work again that night. Yet again, the team experienced bizarre technology blips in the Cabin. The battery power on the camera momentarily jumped up in recording time, which the investigators thought was odd. That was the only room in any of the buildings at the Centre where the team experienced technical anomalies.

Brenda sat to conduct the experiments in the Cabin, and she noticed her legs getting cold. She supposed a window might have been open, but none were. As in the Oppertshauser House, the questions garnered little response until they asked, "Do you not like the gentleman's presence here tonight?" They were referring to their team member Brian, who had a booming voice. The EMF reader lit up brightly.

Ghost Tour

I woke up the morning of my first ghost tour at the Multicultural Heritage Centre with an epiphany. I was reflecting on the popularity of these types of tours and experiences: haunted houses, spooky fun parks, Halloween festivities, cemetery visits, tarot card readings, and meetings with psychics. Some might even group aliens, angels, and religion into this category of otherworldly encounters.

I realised that all these phenomena require a belief in what cannot be seen—and faith in the validity of our own experiences. As Carrie Poppy had said, this is our inner truth that cannot always be verified or understood by others, although that doesn't make it any less real for us.

I continued to ponder. Why are people drawn to supernatural encounters? The answer that popped into my head was simply this:

**Encounters with the dead
make us feel alive.**

Paranormal experiences cause our hearts to race or even skip a beat and we become aware of our mortality. Our skin tingles—all our senses, in fact, are aroused. It is the awareness that there is more going on in our world than only what we can see in the physical realm and conceive of with our rational minds.

Most of us live rather conventionally. We have families and home responsibilities. We go to work, engage in hobbies or other pastimes in the evenings or on weekends, and then the routine begins again come Monday. Encountering ghosts, energies, angels, orbs, and the like snaps us out of our mundane. We begin to wonder what becomes of us after death. We become aware of the energy in our homes and workplaces, and the energy of the living people we encounter—and perhaps the energy of the dead, too.

Some believe that the spirits of deceased relatives protect them or pass on important lessons or messages from their lives before they died or from their afterlife. Others are adamant that guardian angels watch over them. Some claim unfriendly hauntings. This reminds me of the 1988 movie *Beetlejuice* where freshly-dead Barbara and Adam Maitland—played by Geena Davis and Alec Baldwin—attempt to scare away the Deetz family who took up residence in their late home.

All this was going through my head, and I was filled with nervous, excited energy. The Centre marketed the tour as "Tarot for Two,". My husband, Aaron, and I carpooled with our friends, married couple Brian and Lenore. While we drove to Stony Plain, we discussed previous ghost tours we had taken and spooky experiences we'd had.

Brian was skeptical of it all. Aaron wasn't sure what he believed. Lenore told us that she was an empath and explained that she takes on the energy around her. "That could be the energy of the room or the energy of the people around me," she explained to me later by text as I was seeking to understand her deeply felt experiences. "I've noticed it more when there is negative, sad, or bad energy as it really takes a toll on me and my mood—I will start to feel 'heavy with emotions,' and it takes me a while to shake the negative energy."

For my part, I have had multiple spooky experiences in the past. For example, when I was a child I once felt overcome by an evil presence while laying in my bed and had to sing myself to sleep. It was one of those times that didn't make sense; on the outside I was fine, but I still remember it vividly to this day. Is there another explanation for what I experienced? I can't think of anything that would explain what I could sense so tangibly in my body. It was probably one of those "inner truth" moments.

As someone who feels attuned to the spiritual side of life, I went into the ghost tour hoping for an encounter. I stood alone in the Oppertshauser House closet. My chest felt tight, but that could easily be from all the stories I'd read and written about. I remembered Angela telling the lore about the suicide, her face growing splotchy-red as she was unable to breathe during her first tour. Was there residual activity in that closet? Was the spirit of the young man reliving his final moments again and again?

The book *Ghost Hunting: The Science of Spirits*, explains how traumatic incidents leave behind strong pockets of energy where the event took place. "The stronger the emotional impact, the bigger the energetic imprint left behind," writes Julie Tremaine. She also explained another type of energy that is not a spirit, but instead is created from the energy people have when they are in a particular location. This phenomenon is called an Egregore.

"When people believe a space is very haunted, and it attracts visitors' intent on ghosts who, over and over, add psychic energy to the space from their belief that they will find something supernatural there—that energy can eventually create a thought-form that can respond like a ghost would, but has more troublesome characteristics."

Perhaps all the stories about the upstairs closet in the Oppertshauser House have manifested the pain, sadness, and despair of the possible suicide into an Egregore of negative energy. Those who visit create what they expect to see there. I don't know about the Egregore, but the general concept that we make our own reality, that if we look for something we will find it—the old self-fulfilling prophesy notion—makes sense to me.

Who knows? What I was sure of was the fact that I felt lighter, happier even, to leave that closet to tour other parts of the house.

The only jump scare I had while on the tour that night was in the basement of the Oppertshauser House. I don't think we were supposed to venture down there, but I was familiar with the space as an employee. The basement was eerily quiet. Dark. Echoing. I turned the old knob to one of the staff washrooms and nearly leapt out of my skin when I opened the door. Stacked boxes stored in the washroom against one wall looked like a creepy shadow—and the toilet was running loudly.

The energy of the tour, and of my husband and our friends, was primed on that chilly autumn evening. The wine and charcuterie snacks were pleasant, but the leaves scratched ominously across the wooden deck of the Oppertshauser House's summer kitchen. The lights were dimmed in the house and the Red Brick School. Aaron and I received a fateful tarot reading.

As we got in the car to leave the Centre that night, the sky was blue-black and sprinkled with stars only those outside of the city can see. The prairie community was sleepy but for a pesky group of teenagers intent on living it up on their skateboards. I was about to chalk it up as a ghost-free evening when Lenore leaned out the window and took a few quick photos of the front of the Oppertshauser House. The top window had white curtains that looked like they were pulled slightly to the side. That wasn't what made us both say, "That's so weird!" however.

One of the pictures, taken a fraction of a second before the other, shows a small white orb in the black space between the window frame and the curtain. This light area is not present in the photo that immediately followed. We wondered aloud, "What is that?"

The event had already concluded for the evening. Others were leaving like us. The Oppertshauser House was locked up. I could tell because the lights were off and the red EXIT sign glowed through the windows, as seen in the photos. I don't have an explanation for the difference between the two pictures. There is definitely something in the window. A ghost? An orb? I doubt I'll ever know for certain.

Photos by Lenore Washuta

About the Multicultural Heritage Centre

The Centre

The Multicultural Heritage Centre celebrates agriculture, heritage, and the rural values of the region. They recognize that local arts, culture, agricultural practices, and economic opportunities play pivotal roles in building our future.

The Society

The Heritage Agricultural Society operates as the Multicultural Heritage Centre and offers a wide range of programs and services, both onsite and in other locations throughout the region. The Society is the recognized leader in the tri-community region in recording, preserving, and celebrating the agricultural heritage and rural values of the region. They engage residents and visitors in the arts, culture, and sustainable agricultural practices.

The Mission

The Heritage Agricultural Society's mission is to engage residents, businesses, governments, community organizations, and visitors as they record, promote, and celebrate the agricultural heritage, culture, and history of the Town of Stony Plain, the City of Spruce Grove, and Parkland County. They develop and deliver creative and innovative programs and services, providing quality experiences focused on our areas of excellence for residents and visitors, and engage in private, public, and philanthropic partnership opportunities.

Historical Resources

The Multicultural Heritage Centre's Archives, and the Wild Rose Library, contain collections reflecting local history and western Canadian pioneer life. The Historical Resource Centre is accessible for research in genealogy, archival photos, regional maps, and audio recordings.

The Art Gallery

The Multicultural Heritage Centre Public Art Gallery promotes local and regional artists. The gallery brings in new exhibits regularly, hosting opening receptions and creating opportunities for the public to meet the artists, learn more about the artworks, and experience the creative process.

Ghost Tours

The Centre offers public and private ghost tours annually in the autumn and private tours year-round by appointment. A guide leads participants through the Red Brick Schoolhouse and Oppertshauser House, sharing the history and lore of the two buildings and their previous occupants.

Treaty 6 Land Acknowledgment

The Multicultural Heritage Centre honours all the many First Nations, Métis, and Inuit whose footsteps have marked these lands for centuries. They acknowledge that the ancestral and traditional lands on which they gather are Treaty 6 territory, a traditional meeting ground for many Indigenous peoples, and in particular their neighbours, Paul First Nation, Enoch Cree Nation, Alexis Nakota Sioux Nation, and Alexander Cree Nation, on whose territory they work, live, and play, and on whose territory they stand.

Location & Contact Information

5411—51 Street, Stony Plain, Alberta, T7Z 1X7
780-963-2777 | www.MultiCentre.org
YouTube Channel: Multicultural Heritage Centre
Instagram: @multicentreab
Facebook: www.facebook.com/MultiCentreAB
Twitter: @multicentreab

Author Acknowledgments

Thank you to everyone who shared their stories with me for *Prairie Spirits*! Thank you to the Multicultural Heritage Centre for entrusting me with the folklore that so many have passed down over the years. Specifically, I offer sincere gratitude to Melissa Hartley, Jodi Frechette, Angela Fetch Muzyka, Sandra Teves, Twyla McGann, Nicole Rees, Erin Greaves, Victoria Marsh, Sal K., and Robin Lillywhite. A big thank you also to Bill Connelly, aka ParanorBill, and to Beth Fowler of The Alberta Paranormal Investigators Society Inc. for sharing their investigations. Big gratitude as well to my amazing editor, Jo Dawyd.

It is incredibly special to encapsulate the paranormal lore of the Centre in one place. I have done my best to include every story presented as entirely and objectively as possible. My sincere hope is that *Prairie Spirits* will be an enjoyable historical record for many years to come—at least until the second edition, as I'm certain more visitors and staff will have eerie encounters that will need preserving.

I am also grateful to my family. They have endured months of dinnertime ghost stories and countless hours where I've been checked-out while reading and learning about the haunted history of the Centre. Many exciting discussions have taken place because of this project and I am thrilled to share the stories with you, dear readers.

Thank you for reading!

— Alexis Marie Chute

Author Bio

Photo by Aaron Chute

Alexis Marie Chute

Alexis Marie Chute is a distinguished artist, filmmaker, art curator, and bestselling author. Her books include the fantasy trilogy *Above the Star, Below the Moon, Inside the Sun*, and her memoir *Expecting Sunshine: A Journey of Grief Healing and Pregnancy After Loss*. Her documentary film, *Expecting Sunshine: The Truth About Pregnancy After Loss*, was screened in Scotland, France, The Netherlands, and across Canada and the United States. Alexis is the Curator at Wild Skies Art Gallery and at the Multicultural Heritage Centre. Her artwork is represented at the Art Gallery of Alberta.

Contact the Author:
Web: www.AlexisMarieChute.com
Email: info@alexismariechute.com
Twitter: @_Alexis_Marie
YouTube Channel: www.youtube.com/AlexisMarieChute
Instagram: @alexismariejoy

Other Books by Alexis Marie Chute

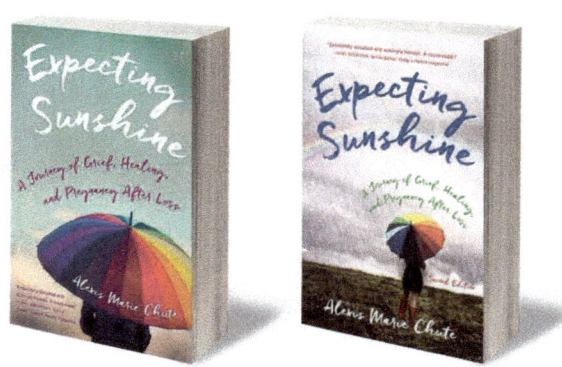

Expecting Sunshine: A Journey of Grief, Healing and Pregnancy After Loss
First and Second Editions

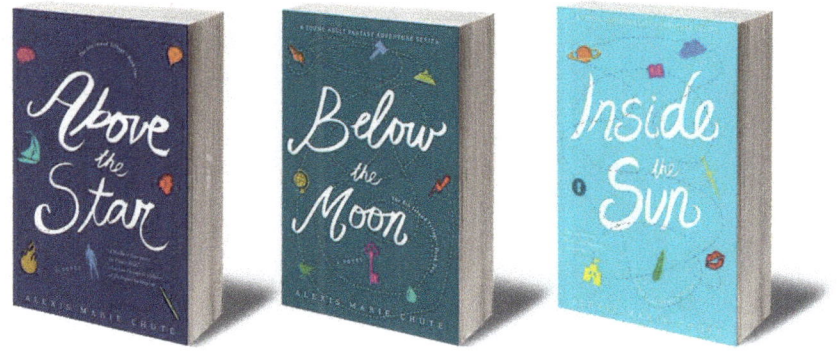

Above the Star, Book one in The 8th Island Trilogy
Below the Moon, Book two in The 8th Island Trilogy
Inside the Sun, Book three in The 8th Island Trilogy

References & Sources

Archives:

Multicultural Heritage Centre records and archives

Books:

Smith, B. (1996). *More Ghost Stories of Alberta*. Lone Pine Publishing.

The Editors of Ghost Hunting. (2021). *Ghost Hunting: The Science of Spirits*. Tandem Books Inc. Meredith Corporation.

Articles:

Sorokan, K. (2017, October 27) "Ghost Tours offer a haunting history" The Grove Examiner. Website: https://www.sprucegroveexaminer.com/2017/10/27/ghost-tours-offer-a-haunting-history

MacDonald, J. (Date Unknown) "Old school has become a leading tourist attraction" Journal. Other details unknown.

YouTube Videos:

The Alberta Paranormal Investigators Society Inc. was founded by Beth Fowler. The society sought to use scientific evidence to investigate paranormal activity. Website: www.albertaparanormal.com, Facebook page: www.facebook.com/AlbertaParanormal, Email: tapis@shaw.ca

TheAlbertaParanormal. (2018, November 8). "Oppertshauser House Paranormal Investigation – Something didn't like one team member." Website: https://www.youtube.com/watch?v=ZTuyiqs5_vw * Full video of the second investigation conducted by The Alberta Paranormal Investigators Society conducted a the Multicultural Heritage Centre in Stony Plain, Alberta, 2012.

TheAlbertaParanormal. (2013, February 16). "Oppertshauser House Investigation - Stony Plain, Alberta." Website: https://www.youtube.com/watch?v=7BmqWm5TeCo (Compilation video of the second investigation conducted by The Alberta Paranormal Investigators Society.)

ParanorBill has been a paranormal researcher and investigator since 1996 and is based in Edmonton, Alberta, Canada. He launched CON-TACT Paranormal Research Investigation and founded the paranormal research facility Haunted Hinsdale House. www.youtube.com/c/paranorbill

Bill ParanorBill Connelly. (2009, September 9). "ParanorBill – Haunted Oppertshauser House Real Paranormal activity caught on tape 1 of 3". Website: https://www.youtube.com/watch?v=dpNvdviUfeU

Bill ParanorBill Connelly. (2009, September 9). "ParanorBill – Haunted Oppertshauser House Real Paranormal activity caught on tape 2 of 3". Website: https://www.youtube.com/watch?v=yMwm7HqbFs8

Bill ParanorBill Connelly. (2009, September 9). "ParanorBill – Haunted Oppertshauser House Real Paranormal activity caught on tape 3 of 3". Website: https://www.youtube.com/watch?v=yVDC2xzfkC4

TED. Ideas worth spreading. (2016, October). "A scientific approach to the paranormal" Carrie Poppy, TEDxVienna. Website: https://www.ted.com/talks/carrie_poppy_a_scientific_approach_to_the_paranormal

Interviews & Firsthand Accounts

Jodi Frechette, Angela Fetch Muzyka, Melissa Hartley, Sandra Teves, Twyla McGann, Nicole Rees, Erin Greaves, Victoria Marsh, Sal K., Robin Lillywhite

Photo, Illustration, & Font Credits

Historical building photos: Multicultural Heritage Centre Archives*, Photographer Unknown.

The Multicultural Heritage Centre's Archives, and the Wild Rose Library, preserve and present collections of images and artifacts—such as records of genealogy, archival photos, regional maps, and audio recordings—of local history, documenting western Canadian pioneer life in the region.

George and Barbara Oppertshauser Portrait: Multicultural Heritage Centre Archives, Photographer Unknown

Cornelia Wood Portrait: Multicultural Heritage Centre Archives, Photographer Unknown

Creative photos & recreations: Alexis Marie Chute

Models: Nicole Rees, Ethan Lang, and Luca Chute

Ghost Tool Illustrations: Alexis Marie Chute, with special thanks to Hannah Chute

Stock: Werner Weisser, Prettysleepy, Darkmoon Art, Pixabay, Free Photos, dre2uomaha0, Gerd Altmann, Gordon Johnson, ipicgr, István Mihály, Open Clipart, Pexels, Tumisu, Sharonjoy17, jakov zadro, Robert Karkowski, Axionate, WikiImages, Comfreak, Chris Martin, Momentmal, Hebi B.

Ghost Tour Photos: Erin Greaves, Victoria Marsh, Lenore Washuta

Cover Font: Beyond Wonderland by Chris Hansen
Chapter Title Font: American Typewriter
Text Font: Times New Roman

www.ingramcontent.com/pod-product-compliance
Lightning Source LLC
Chambersburg PA
CBHW061154010526
44118CB00027B/2967